For most people, dande[lions are a nuisance] and nothing more than [an invasive weed. But to] Theresia Elder, they are an expression of her life experiences and a manifestation of God's marvelous work. The charming poems she penned could be interpreted and read as modern psalms, expressing the author's relationship with God with themes of joy and exultation, wonder and struggle, and praise and thanksgiving.

Dandelions are a humble weed, transforming plain fields into a blanket of yellow. They can be used to make wine; in seed form, they delight children who make wishes and scatter the seedlings with their breath. There is more to the humble dandelion than meets the eye, and the poetry in this book warmly reflects the author's struggles, joyful faith, hopeful outlook and creative view of all things God has created, even the humble dandelion.

—Rev. David Wilhelm, Chaplain,
Our Lady Queen of Peace Monastery,
Hamilton, Ontario. Canada

Dandelion EXPERIENCES

POETIC PRAYERS FOR A WINDY DAY

SISTER THERESIA ELDER RPB

Sr Theresia

Printed in Canada

ISBN: 978-1-4866-2485-0
eBook ISBN: 978-1-4866-2486-7

Word Alive Press
119 De Baets Street Winnipeg, MB R2J 3R9
www.wordalivepress.ca

Cataloguing in Publication information can be obtained from Library and Archives Canada.

Dedicated to the

One

who sees beyond
my dandelions.

Contents

Acknowledgement

WITH DEEP GRATITUDE, I wish to thank Sister Gisèle Goguen RPB, General Superior of the Sisters of the Precious Blood, for permitting me to publish my Poetry and for her encouragement in this venture.

Also deserving of my gratitude are the many people who read this poetry and suggested that I publish it.

This project could never have been possible without the tremendous help of Father Dave Wilhelm, who has journeyed with me in every stage of the publication.

Foreword

When on a lawn quite green
Some dandelions do show,
It's a detested weed
That simply must not grow.

When in the tiny hands
Of one who loves and cares,
The dandelion now flowers
Into a gift one shares.

The dandelion is a weed?
Ah! Take another look
And journey now with me
Into my precious book.

Just One Flame of Love

Am I on the Magic Carpet,
Or sailing on Cloud Nine?
In this view I see all creation
With eyes that are not mine.

The earth rings out in joy
As it bursts into new songs.
For all of God's creation
I get a sense that it belongs.

How is it that I see things
I've never seen before?
As the trees no longer walk
And splinters fall to the floor.

How I long to do things for others.
As for jobs, it does not matter.
I even would have served
Right into a dancing platter.

I sing, I dance, and I twirl
like one happy child
Falling in love with the Lord—
can anything tend to be mild?

Fling open the cloister door;
let all the people come in,
For here in a heavenly banquet
It is love that purifies sin.

The Call of the Bridegroom

Theresia, I announce to you
I want you for my Bride.
I pledge to you my faithful love
Within you to abide.

This ring shall be the symbol of
Our love in giving all,
For faithfulness look thus to Me,
Especially when you fall.

Jesus, I take Thee for my Spouse
And pledge exclusive love.
I call as witness to this vow
God and the Saints above.

To love Thee! Oh! To love Thee, Lord!
Let this song be the hymn
I want to sing eternally,
In love to Thee Belong.
(written at eighteen years of age)

My Umbrella World

Pulled together
like a closed accordion,
locking in the potential
to expand
in notes of joy,
tightly drawn,
I protectively walk
in the rain.
Squish, squash,
I step on a worm.
It shouldn't have been on the sidewalk,
in my way, anyway.
I step off: it is lifeless,
and the same feeling knots me inside.
In my umbrella journey
I hardly notice the wet face
passing me.
After all, it is raining!
I do not stop
to close the flood gates—
that may mean getting wet.
I enter my house so perfectly dry.

But O Lord, WHAT A BIG DRIP AM I.

Quid Retribuam

O what can I give Thee, Father,
For all Thou art giving to me?
O what can I give Thee, Jesus,
For all Thou art giving to me?
O what can I give Thee, Spirit,
For all Thou art giving to me?

For the life that comes in abundance
As moments of grace set me free ...
For the call of a loving friendship
Wherein I am coming to be ...
For the frequent inspirations
in lights that help me to see.
BY THE VOICE OF THE
BLOOD OF JESUS
I will praise thee eternally.

Ring Out Ye Bells

My heart overflows with a noble theme
As I sing my ode to the King.
My tongue, be like a faithful scribe
Thy praises all to sing!

As grace is poured into my heart
My lips His love proclaim
While blessings in abundance flow,
Each torch I long to flame!

I leave my people and my home
To turn my gaze above.
But bring them all to this great feast;
I need more hearts to love!

For God, my God, has poured on me
The oil of gladness too.
My BRIDAL SONG bursts forth in love,
I do, I do, I DO!

(Written on the occasion of my Perpetual Profession of Vows,
based on Psalm 45)

Faith

Faith is a journey into the unknown
believing in Someone else:
I BELIEVE
in the constant action of God ·
Who creates this day.
I believe
in His faithful, enduring love,
which freely comes my way.
I BELIEVE
in Christ, the Incarnate One,
whose friendship is so real.
I believe
that He makes His home in me
in a presence I can feel.
I BELIEVE
in the Spirit's energy, who
is making all so new with care.
I believe
in the Spirit's creative touch,
which makes the earth a house of prayer.

I BELIEVE
IN THE LOVE THE SPIRIT IS!!!

Lord, Send My Roots Rain

As a tiny sheaf of wheat,
I seek His life and light.
I glory in refreshing air
And in the sun so bright.

But when it does not rain
My roots get thirsty-weak.
My feelers I then must plunge
In depths I search and seek.

It's in these depths I learn
That sun and rain and air
A wealth of meaning hold
In my Father's loving care.

Our Peach Tree

Beside our small car-less garage
There stood a fruitless tree.
The soil was greatly to be blamed—
That we could clearly see!

Each year the leaves were less and less,
The blossoms fewer still.
And oh! the peaches that we sought,
No basket would they fill.

One day our neighbour telephoned:
"Oh Sister, did you know?
Your withered little peach tree crashed
Onto the lane below."

Unlike this withered tree, Oh Lord,
Grant that my life may be
Like to the tree at water's edge,
Producing FRUITFULLY.

(Inspired by Psalm 1)

Becoming Wholeness

There are no moments to be compared
With the ones I have shared
When in the stillness of presence resting,
My love grows in deep questing.
In the shadow of my heart
A lasting miracle has a start.
Fewer are formalities;
Now bursting are realities:
The reality of my God, Yahweh.
The reality of self on its way.
Each time He comes to me
I gradually BEGIN TO BE ...
In this continuous state of Becoming
With diminishing hallucinations
I've come to learn love's alternations:
Love that will inflame and unfold,
Love whose feelings are quite cold ...
Love's story is never fully told
Until it becomes a FIRE-gold.

Lead, Kindly Light

Lead, kindly Light, lead me on,
For a call I have heard.
Lead me into the depths
of the Living Word.

Lead, kindly Light, lead me on
To surrender all to you.
Lead me to let go to all
that to myself is not true.

Lead, kindly Light, lead me on,
In the clarity of sight.
Lead me, for my glass-visioned
eyes make for a dim light.

Lead, kindly Light, lead me on.
Gladly with you have I trod.
Lead me into the Eternal
Wisdom of my God.

(Inspired by the words of John Henry Newman
"Lead, Kindly Light")

Touched by Him

Precious the sacred moment
When I encounter you!
Enfolded within Your Being
My true self comes to view.

**O Solitude,
I need you to proclaim His presence.**

Within the sacred silence
While called to go apart,
You enfold within Your Being
Loved creatures of Your heart.

**O my people,
I need you to proclaim His love.**

I need to go the extra mile ...
I need to wash Your sacred feet.
I need to quench Your thirst
And from all pagan love retreat.

Into my frail and sinful clay
You breathe Your life anew.
I know with joyful certainty
That I've encountered You.

**Praise and thanks, Lord,
for the gift of Your Being!**

DANDELION EXPERIENCES

The Nelson Bus Station

The celebrant was quite late,
So the morning Mass was late.
And I was late, and in this situation
In getting to the bus station.

Rush, rush, rush!
Yet! Telling my heart to hush!

Amidst this rush there was no room for seclusion.
A lady came to me in great confusion;
The lady pleaded with me, in a spirit rather low,
"I have all day at this station. Where can I go?"

As my time-frame is all in a blur,
I could not find time for her,
So in an apologetic voice,
"I'm late for my bus. I just have no choice."

I rush to the waiting bus driver,
And now question all I've deprived her.
In closing the door between us,
I journey in darkness on this bus.

For an important specialist appointment,
I journey in great disappointment.
For as I go to another city,
All day long I remain at that bus station, in pity.

To the Nelson bus station, in the evening, I return,
And the lady is still sitting there, I learn.
Her bus just arrived, and I watch and pray
That many, many blessings will come her way.

I sometimes wonder and know it's hard to say,
Which of us had the most difficult day.

Nelson, B.C., February 13, 1969

His Searching Word

The Sower went out to sow ...
   —In the city noise
   —His Word keeps searching for me
   —To the wilderness
   —It leads and draws
There, in a fearful, disturbing silence

   I talk, talk,
      I chatter-talk.

   THE SEEDLESS EARTH
   IS WATERED AND SUNNED.

Some seed fell among thorns ...
I hurry back to the city
Only to find
   —that the walls are down;
   —that my trained warriors have been slain;
   —that I can no longer find my own door.

   I cry, I cry
      I questioningly cry.

   THE WIND BLOWS
   THE TOP SOIL.

   Some seed fell on good soil ...

Again and again,
I face the wilderness
As words begin to nestle
in the silent furrows of my heart.

I ponder, I ponder,

I Mary-ponder

THE GENTLE RAIN SHOWERS.
THE WHEAT WAVES ITS GREEN.

They come back rejoicing, carrying their sheaves ...

A new city I enter:
—lights are everywhere. I SEE.
—water is gently flowing
-through the city. I GROW.
—fruit trees are lifting their
—laden arms in praise. I AM IN HIM.

THE LAMB BREAKS THE SEVENTH SEAL
AND THERE WAS SILENCE ...

THE GOLDEN HARVEST.

In a relaxed presence of silence

Fulfilling and overpowering,
His WORD abides
Enriching my soil
He brings HIS WORD to my silent wonder
He brings silence to my words.

> *"I am the bread of life," says Jesus.*

Psalm of Praise

Let His Word go forth;
Let us praise Him for His concrete love.
We, as the people of the Lord!

His Word is seeking Incarnation,
searching deep in the soul.
Painful eruption
penetrating division of a two-edged sword.

A confrontation eliminating
checker passivity,
bringing life and direction into our lives,
as we accept His Word.

Others may have their mute idols;
Ours is a living and life-giving God
in constant self-revelation.

He spoke, and creation began.
God initiates order,
Chaos now emerging into unity
as our creative function takes shape.

Fathers of old transmit the message
of the Word.
Prophetic men too unfold the salvific plan.

Mary believes in the Word,
expands and grows in this dynamic reality.
A daughter of Abraham, she hears
the message and it becomes a living power.

God speaks to us through His Son,
Jesus, the living revelation of the Father,
in whom we have salvation.

Through the Word we gradually move
toward a total, unifying love.
We open ourselves to that love which is the TRINITY.

As in the parable of the sower,
We receive His Word uniquely,
In everyone, and each one personally.

It is seeking Incarnation.
We hear, we understand, we accept.
We seek to keep it faithfully in a fruitful life.

LET HIS WORD GO FORTH.
LET US PRAISE HIM FOR HIS CONCRETE LOVE—
WE AS THE PEOPLE OF THE LORD!

The Great Escalator

Emerging steps ascend and disappear,
Transporting people all day long. And I?
Just stood there with great fears enchained. To try
This new way, no toil involved. "Why Fear?"
My father's pleading voice now reached my ear.
"I can't," I told him with a frightened cry.
His hands reached out: I felt all knots untie.
Now on that step, I could go on from here.

Who shall ascend the Mount of God above?
When love has smothered out all fear and fright,
I feel His drawing; slowly I let go
And journey on His escalating love!
While lifted in a steady upward flight,
My heart expands in love I did not sow.

Lost in the Beloved

When machines and robots were publicized
We were told we'd have lots of time on hand.
Life on the Lakeshore was soon in the planning
While dreaming of a world that looked so grand.
But when the machines began taking over
We became aware that we had a new boss.
And it did not take long until we realized
Our time for leisure was at a great loss.

Consumerism/materialism and productivity,
In a few years, went right out of line.
Many lives were feeling the emptiness,
For this all added to the pressure of time.

The social utility calls us to be very useful,
Especially when the activists are strong.
The idea of taking any amount of leisure
Was sure to be labelled as wrong.

But we are not just materially made,
For the restless heart expresses a need
To take some leisure with our God
And to all His teaching take heed.

People are always at a racing speed,
Even to the sound of screeching tires,
While the contemplatives sit in silent prayer
With hearts full of burning desires.

I praise and thank You, O Father,
For the hours that I have been blest
In leisure with my Beloved Lord,
Uniting this to Your Sabbath rest.

A Temple Prayer

The Pharisee inside of me takes a stand.
My prayers I proclaim as a life most grand.

I am more than generous with every gift—
A tenth I offer, giving others a lift.

I fast and make sure all the rules apply,
And from a life of penance, I do not shy.

As for sinners, like the one back there,
I just keep a distance, for I really don't care.

Ah! Take note! You're standing on holy ground,
Where saints and sinners can both be found.

Your sins you cannot restrain inside,
But find ways to plague the sinners outside.

It is said, BUT for the grace of God go I.
Just pray in humble identity and cry,

There go I.

Fill the Jars

Spirit of God look on your re-creation,
Shaped for our task and our purpose in life.
Help us respond to this invitation:

**Fill the jars
Right to the brim
And draw some out now
Pressed down
Overflowing
The work of the Spirit
Breathing within.**

Vessel of clay, we hold gifts in all frailness.
Easily shattered, we're often afraid.
Let's celebrate Your strength in our weakness ...

**Fill the jars
Right to the brim.**

To receive You is my deep yearning essence,
Constantly pouring out what we've received,
Always renewed in Your peaceful presence.

**Right to the Brim ...
Fill the jars**

If in our life there's growing fulfillment
Changing of water into rich wine
It is the Spirit in love's our-movement.

**Fill the jars
Right to the brim ...**

Denken ist Danken

We thank the God of peace and love
Whenever we think of you:
To Him and to each other you
Have striven to be true.

On this your celebrated day
We pray for nothing less
Than blessings that will activate
A deeper faithfulness.

And may these blessings richly flow
Out through each generation
Jacob, Franz, Jordan,
Elizabeth, Mary, Katherine,
Julia, Theresia, Karl, & Margaret.
As you live on in each of us
Through loving imitation.

As happily we gather now
A witness to your love
We THINK of all you've done for us
And THANK God above.

(On the occasion of my parents'
fiftieth wedding anniversary, June 17, 1973)

My Whispered Answer

I gathered a large bouquet for my lover.
Carefully, I arranged each flower,
Making sure that the roses were in full view.
Graciously, He accepted my offering,
As He picked from my floral arrangement
A sheaf of wheat, which to me
shall always of our union a symbol be.

"This is My Body.
Come, in My banquet of joy share."

Then He took a red rose with such delicate care;

"This is My Blood,
My suffering, My Love.
Come, follow Me."

He picked a bright yellow rose and said,

"You see, the joys we share in these are met,"
As He placed it with the wheat
and the rose blood-red.

Horrified!

I saw Him take a dandelion.
In His hand the full yellow turned fluff white.

With a gentle breeze from His lips,
He blew the white stuff away.
T'was then my heart
heard the most wonderful sound:

**"Here," He whispered,
"Is our MEETING GROUND.**

**All the flowers you brought to Me
hold meaning
In your dandelions, which you
from Me have been screening."**

No longer ashamed,
I presented all my dandelions:
The heart-breaking, fragile,
Thinness, and poverty of my love
and of my prayer.
At that moment—or was it a moment?
As He blew each lion away,
How dandy!
He blows the "im" from impossible,
Calling my Christian strength
forth into life like the white fluff
reaching out, searching for renewal
in His creative soil,

To begin a new dimension of love.

Let There Be Life

A rose-bud nipped in a field of plenty.
A womb life-pregnant is aborted empty.
The world proclaims it has no room
As life that ends in a garbage tomb.

Teach us, O Lord, Your concerns to share
For life you're creating in such delicate care.

A face-covered stretcher is carried by;
People are angry and bitterly cry,
"It's cruel, untimely and most unfair;
This God of ours, He does not care."

Lord, we take upon ourselves, it's true,
The very rights that we deny you!

(Written after seeing a face-covered stretcher brought up a
mountainside after a day of Concern for Life, 1979)

Journey in Freedom

Are these Your words I am hearing,
Which my heart now questions, while fearing?

"Take these words; I offer no disguises.
Use for your journey as the need arises.
Go forth, leave all,
On your journey depart.
I mean to deliver you
From the Egypt of your heart."

Lord, You've got to be kidding!
I can't understand Your bidding.
But then,
I do saunter out ...
and whom do you think I meet?
I journey with Him on eagle's wings,
For freedom stumbles with feet.

My Moses Tree

I walk into my garden of solitude.
Thoughts like the still, clear waters rest in my heart.
I've come so often before to be with my Gardener.

In the touch of Presence I am brought to a halt
Before my flaming tree!
The closer I go in search of the beyond,
The further the flame journeys.
My fruitless efforts bring me low.

In loving stillness I abide.
I take off my shoes, and before the Great Flame,
I bend in adoration and surrender,
To receive the all-consuming fire of love.

A treasured moment of infused Flame.
I no longer behold the flame tree before me.
I journey in a presence not mine;
I walk with a Flame not mine.
Yet what could be more mine?

**"In Me you live and move
and have your being."**

He speaks His Word to my experiences.
I come to understand my experiences through His Word.

Beyond the Sign

In an atmosphere of smog, I await
For bus connections, I debate
How best to use the time
In this the clime
Of blear.

I feel myself encircled in a pace
Of crowds and noise; as people race,
I long for quiet peace
Or some release
From here.

From the rushing crowd, I'm greeted;
Soon waiting hours are deleted.
Now time goes racing by
As someone's cry
I hear.

In search of God whom did they find but me.
My religious sign was just that key
For our paths to meet
On this packed street.
So queer!

Your call to witness is my gift; I feel
My sense of mission sparks so real.
The cloister and this place
Have one love-face
All year.

By the Voice of Your Blood

A tree of abundant life
stands in the name of all creation.
Its extended branch-arms
are constantly lifted in prayer-praise.

"Holy, holy, holy
is the Lord of creation!"

All earth chants beneath the tree.
Gradually the crimson leaves
trickle gently to the ground.
A pleading voice goes forth:

"Redeem Your people, Lord."

The last leaves fall at midday
from the tree already winter dead.
In the spring of new life,
branches we become
and in the fruitfulness of the Tree, we cry:

"You have redeemed us, Lord,
in Your Blood. Alleluia"

God's Re-Creating Friendship

God seeks to be a loving friend.
In Covenant He seals
A friendship He alone can form,
While secrets He reveals.
Love communicated.

"Of you is my praise in the thronged assembly"
(Psalm 22:25a).

*"May the words of my mouth always find favour, and
the whispering of my heart, in your presence, Yahweh,
my rock, my redeemer"* (Psalm 19:14).

Each time He encounters me,
My roots for depth do seek,
And in the joy of union blessed,
His love my heart does reap.
Exhilarating Oneness

*"Let the light of your face shine on us. Yahweh, to my
heart, you are a richer joy than all their corn and new
wine"* (Psalm 4:7).

*"May my musings be pleasing to him, for Yahweh gives
me joy"* (Psalm 104:34).

There comes a time of leaving all,
The call to simply TRUST.
I journey forth, not without fears,
Of being stripped to dust.
The Tense Unknown

*"By the rivers of Babylon we sat and wept at the
memory of Zion"* (Psalm 137:1).

"God, hear my cry, listen to my prayer" (Psalm 61:1).

I wander in a wilderness,
With stumbling feet I go.
While in my circles I now meet,
A much unwanted foe.

Life's Superficial Knowledge

*"He sees himself with too flattering an eye to detect
and detest his guilt"* (Psalm 36:2).

"I made my sin known to you, did not conceal my guilt"
(Psalm 32:5a).

It's autumn in the forest now;
The leaves must all be shed.
And in the stripping, letting go,
Our friendship is then wed.

Striving Toward Inward Realities

"You have pierced all his defenses, and laid his strongholds in ruins" (Psalm 89:40).

"You have stripped him of his splendid sceptre, and toppled his throne to the ground" (Psalm 89:44).

A burning light keeps drawing me,
To where a clearing free
Will bring me to the vision of
One LOVE, of depth in THREE.

Shattered My Glass Vision

"My whole being yearns and pines for Yahweh's courts, My heart and my body cry out for joy to the living God" (Psalm 84:2).

"Even the sparrow has found a home" (Psalm 84:3a).

No Upward Web

With a secure attachment
A spider let go from the ceiling.
In true spider fashion
I sometimes let go, but feeling
my way along in fear,
always checking
that my security is near.

The spider web then dangles,
As though at the end of its rope.
And I, in silence,
ponder the meaning of hope.

The poor little creature
landing now in my sink,
Struggles desperately and in vain.
But I now think:
I can in an upward web
my freedom gain in a wink!

For your precious gift of
Christian Hope,
I praise You, Lord.

The Father Will Dance

"Hurry down,
I mean to stay in your house."

Down, down we venture
into the still regions of my house,
past the sparkling, spotless rooms
and into the dark, messy rooms.

TODAY,

I WANT Him to see everything.
I mean everything.
I want Him to see the dirt, the mess,
and the emptiness I feel in some parts of my house.
We linger in these rooms.
Why am I showing these to Him?

I feel ashamed, yet I really want Him
to see everything. I mean everything!
That seems so extremely important.
It really is His house.
Many years ago, on the 7th of September,
He brought it into existence
and then took possession of it on the 20th.

He made His home in it.
It was so completely His!
But in my sinfulness, I began to lay claims,
to build sin walls and barriers,
and these became rooms.

All these years I sought to keep Him
mostly in the spotless, sparkling rooms.
When I did show Him various things
from the dark, dirty rooms,
I would take these things out of their rooms
and bring them to Him one by one.

I had always hoped that
He would not care to even look.
But just in case He did,
I would try to remove some of the dirt.
I would cover over some of the rips and stains,
doing all I could so it would not look so bad.

But TODAY,

I want Him to see everything.
I mean everything!
I wanted him to see it
just as it really is.
He looked with compassion and concern
that I should have been living in such a mess,

for it was so unnecessary.
With raised hand He said,
"I absolve you from all your sins."

My sparkling, spotless rooms
and my dark, dirty rooms
became as one house
where we made ourselves at home completely.
And the music of the home praised Him!
I fell into His arms
and we danced, and danced, and danced.

For
"Salvation has come to his house today."

Celebrating the Eucharist

I keep bringing
bits of knowledge to Him.
Fragments, I keep gathering.

It's strange!
The loaf awaits my pieces
to make again the perfect whole.

His hand raised in blessing
over the loaf
gives coherence and a unity
to the One united whole.

With new convictions
I go forth,
constrained and impelled
into His saving Action.

God's Yeasting Love

Please accept,
Lord, our bread,
Always in the fresh making,
Working for
Moments when
More is ready for baking.
Kneading it well
And then watching it swell,
Brim into its fullness.
Silently,
Gradually
In His yeasting love rising.

Baking it,
Breaking it,
Christians loving and sharing.
Give to all.
Heed the call,
For the multitude caring.
Strength is renewed
And the heart made new
In each great awaking,
Recognize,
Once again,
Christ as in the BREAD BREAKING.

Anamnesis (Memorial)

Christ has died
O PAST—I let you go freely
and with my blessings,
for truly you have been a blessing to me.

Christ is Risen

O PRESENT—I live in the Bread of now,
so full of life and so sacrificial,
calling forth a new self-giving.
Bread, reverently slipping from
his consecrated fingers
into the chalice.

May this mingling of the Body and Blood of
Jesus Christ bring the Risen Lord to life in us ...

"Christ will come again."

O FUTURE! In your hands I am being formed
constantly in the act of creation:
you urge me,
you compel me,
you challenge me forth.

"May almighty God bless you,
in the name of the Father,
and of the Son, and
of the Holy Spirit.
GO IN THE PEACE OF CHRIST."

I Need to Sing of Your Love

I feel the burden of the planks in my eye,
Then the vision of the others I can't unify.

I feel my temple is often cluttered.
How can that possibly be?

GOD ALONE!!! I hear this cry so pleadingly.

I feel the darkness in so much of my praying,
All those words I just keep on slaying.

The sky opens! The wind blows all this clutter away,
And the water cleanses, leaving a rainbow to stay.

All is clean! So very sacramentally clean,
And a new beginning is clearly seen.

Freedom & inspiration in abundance flow.
Sadly, it will be messed again, that I know.

Realizing with joys so rich and new,
Please, do not deprive me of my deep need of YOU.

I NEED TO SING OF YOUR LOVE!

The Jonah in Me

His message echoes in my frightened,
tightened heart, through which
it cannot freely, clearly go forth.
Struggles my heart with its octopus outlets,
strained and overloaded.
Out goes the fuse!
And I?
Sit darkened in narrow-minded miseries
and map-folding confusion.

THE JONAH TUGS IN ME.
I'LL RUN FROM IT ALL AND BE FREE!

But chains, chains—
Attitudes chains, platitude chains.
Non-concentrated forces march out,
While non-penetrated depths are left gaping.
Like an autumn leaf so little holds me—
Easily I come down,
down ...

Wind-blown or just a breeze ...
Then in a Jonah flight
with thoughtless speed
to the ends of the earth I travel.

Sea-bound, all but drowned
in evasive escapes and non-committals,
swallowed by the monster
lurking in the gap
of what I'd like to be and am,
whenever I stand before IDENTITY.

The Jonah tugs in me.
I'll run from it all and be free!

Cast on the shore
where my escape had begun,
I fall, restless, soggy, and wet,
pasted to the ground
in a rotting darkness,
yet in potential enrichment.
Lord, in spite of these escapes,
Your message trickles through:
There is just no escaping you!

The Jonah tugs in me.
Lord, teach me how to be free!

Hymn to Christ—Eucharist

A new melody
Prays on the strings of my being
With sounds of transformation.

Each day at the
Table of the Eucharist
this melody swells and brims
in love desires.

Within Your Sacred Hands
The moments are blessed when I come
As Bread and wine before You,
longing to be transformed.

"This is My Body."
Take, eat, and in love feed my sheep.
"This is My Blood."
Take, drink, and in union
Channel Its life-flow.

How often as I go I see
The table of the Eucharist
And feel the need to break bread.
I share Eucharist
And become Eucharist
As His Word consecrates my life.

Love Him for Us

Gently, the Gospel Word goes out,
Bringing excitement to my heart,
Which burns in love and desire,
As from the chapel I depart.

Lightly, my feet now wing me forth
To calls of duty for the day,
As with the Gospel woman
My heart sings on its way.

I longed for her astounding faith,
Which she before the Saviour brought.
We shared the day into the night
While I this treasure from Him sought.

As morning dawns another day,
Again the path of faith I tread,
But heavy in my heart now lies
The fact that my dear dad is dead.

While faith with questions probe my heart,
Deep love and sorrow swell inside.
A loneliness creeps in, tears join
The rain I can no longer hide.

"I am the Resurrection."
I hear, I understand and see.
As He proclaims this life to Dad,
He also brings a new life to me.

"O woman, you have such great faith,
Your wish shall come to pass," said He.
My being prayed but one request,
"MY GOD, LOVE DAD ETERNALLY!"

Burning Incense

In its quiet depths
Someone put incense
into the thurible of my heart,
and a prayer ascended
that was not mine.

O Word of God,
I am not worthy
that You should use my temple,
my sinful temple,
for your prayer to the Father.

I Need to Proclaim His Love!

He loves me! A new life began
As from the cross He bridged the span
Of all that could keep us apart.
He arrows deeply in my heart,
A love that He alone could fan.
This loving melody now ran
In all I seek to be and am:

How good Thou art! How great Thou art!
He loves me!

This inward journey has a plan
That's rooted in the God-made Man.
The lives of others are a part
Of this love-journey He did start.
To love and take all in His scan.
He loves me!

How good Thou art! How great Thou art!
He loves me!

He loves me! My heart longs to tell
How I met Him at Jacob's well.
A friend asked for a drink; I knew
The well went into that plea too!
I'll always thirst with Him to dwell.

And in my heart began to swell
A song of faith that love could tell
was stirred by Him, and I just knew
He loves me!

**How good Thou art! How great Thou art!
He loves me!**

Faith moments of resistance fell
Upon my heart, but would these gel?
He pleaded, "If you only knew
the gift of self I'm offering you."
I dropped my needs into the well.
He loves me!

**How good Thou art! How great Thou art!
He loves me!**

He loves me! What a precious place,
The synagogue held a special grace.
As He proclaimed Himself t'was clear
My Mary stance could burst forth here.
A silent gaze upon your face,
I find a way out of this maze,
And my whole being changed its pace.
I drew so near, so very near.
He loves me!

How good Thou art! How great Thou art!
He loves me!

My life is yours always, always
To surrender and to embrace.
All that I could ever dread or fear
Could keep from me thus drawing near.
In an adoring love-filled gaze.
He loves me!

Icon Prayer

I feel Your Triune gaze,
Your gentle, loving scrutiny,
Your purifying, holy gaze,
penetrating the bread and wine
of my questing being,
longing to be TRANSFORMED.

In this beholding,
seeking eternal identity,
a thousand words are lost in its depths.

Your gaze, so personal,
so immensely personal,
contains and embraces all
within the cup of crucified love.
You so long to make my life this cup
as I daily journey
to Your Holy Table.

Loved, challenged, and purified,
I know that I've been gazed into!

O Praise!

O praise of the heavens
Penetrate earth
And to more praise
In this union give birth!

O praise where the presence
Of God makes holy
And in all that lives
just to praise God only.

O praise into the dark
Places of sin;
Find Your entrance
and redemption bring.

O praise in the cymbals,
The harp, and the lute;
Let not your praise
In these sounds be mute.

O praise in all creatures,
In birds and trees,
And in everything living
In whom life breathes.

Yes, everyone, everything
simply must praise
Until earth and heaven
this one hymn raise.

O PRAISE!

(Inspired by Psalm 150)

Invitation and Inspiration

Ant: "Come to the Banquet of Plenty
The Lord will provide all that you need.
Come to the Banquet of Plenty"
(Psalm: Special occasion of letting go!)

I am your God,
your faithful God with a heart of friendship and love.
I, your God, heard your cry
to deliver you from the Egypt enslaving your prayer.

Come! Let us go to the mountain
where a sacrificial banquet is summoning us.
It will mean total involvement,
not just participation.
Bread and wine will be served;
no gods are to travel with you.

My companion gods circle round
Like weeping willows that tower over me.
I make my round and dismiss these gods of mine,
When I do so, Behold! A surprise awaits me!

The Lord has entered the circle.
He has always been there.
I did not notice Him, for my gods distract me.

Newness now sparks my journey
As He maps our way to the banquet,
the Sacrificial Banquet on the Mountain.

DANDELION EXPERIENCES

Song of Grace

A natural vacancy
addresses my heart
in an emptiness and a void
that stretches toward You, O God,
for its only true fullness.

Even in chaotic slavery
my heart awaits
the power and action
of the Holy Spirit
and searches for
depth in You, Creator God.

Behold! Then into my heart
You so powerfully erupt
until in a volcano action
pour out Your love
into the abyss of Who You are,
O my God.

What Makes Me Apostolic

In a Spirit-movement
changing into depths the ripples of my life,
I've come to know the ocean of His love.
The voice of the Lord sounded over the water:

"Whom shall I send?
Whom shall I send to preach the Gospel,
to baptize, to proclaim redemption
through the power of the Blood of Jesus
and His Spirit?"

I responded enthusiastically,
"Send me, Send ME, SEND ME!"

With a Father's love,
He gifted me with a conch.
I sat for what seemed like an eternity
at the water's edge,
with my conch pressed tightly
against the concha of my heart, until
in the depth I heard a hallowed sound
and understood my mission:

"Abba, Father,"
the Spirit prayed deep within.

The Darkness of Attachments

Many DARKENED COLOURS
On my canvas I have brushed,
Leaving forms and images
Either blurred or hushed.

I quickly brush in colours
Of yellow, blue, and red,
But black streaks keep appearing
With the heaviness of led.

Each time You come and splash
A nada darkness on your Bride,
An attachment is then silenced
And my "Fiat" purified.

I praise you for the darkness

Bringing value to the light,
For the pure, unbroken forces
Of the Spirit's love—delight!

Filling Now with the Eternal

"I am here," says the Lord,
And sometimes you are there.
But it's only in one place
We communicate in prayer.

Thoughts sail in a dreamy future
Or saunter in a lifeless past;
Most of these land in a limbo,
While meditation is a task.

In an invasion of distraction
Your mind goes many places.
Just unwind into awareness
And receive a flow of graces.

Let Me lead you to a holy place
Where "I Am" abides therein,
Where the **present** is a sacrament
That touches everything.

Sursum Corda!
Yes, lift up you heart and soul
To the Presence of God everywhere.
In the Lord's Eucharistic Presence
There's just nothing to compare.

I will live in the Presence
of the Lord, in the land of the living!

A Parable

He said, "Imagine a sower going out to sow."
Imagine an ARTIST going out to sculpt,
seeking for essence in form.
As he sculpted, some marble resisted
the drive of his chisel, so much
that along with his unfinished work,
there were many chips and pieces for
terrazzo flooring and stucco houses,
but not the image he longed to form.

Other marble took to formation,
but later the image was ruined because
the acid preparation had penetrated too deeply.
The image was there but discoloured and disfigured,
and thus not too pleasing to the artist.

Other marble was rich in quality.
It seemed to exist only to
await the touch of the Artist.
With integrity and totality of thought
he FORMED HIS IMAGE.
Compelled to create depth,
he chiselled and polished away.
The marble vibrated with life! BEHOLD!

The TRIUNE dimensional image
Knows the joys of a hundred-fold.

Visits to the Pool

I've come before
to this place of healing.
I envision that in its great movement,
the healing powers lie.

How is it that I wait so long to be placed therein?
Yes, long have I grown weary of asking
the passer-by to help me in.

Someone does stop!
He understandingly says,
"Do you want ..."

In the waiting silence,
I turn my eyes upon Him;
I wonder why the pool attracted me so!
In His eyes I see
a thousand pools of healing and of hope.

I realized today
that He has stopped before.
Pools, I muse, have a way of distracting me.

But before He could complete
His sentence, I did.
"Yes, I want to go into the pool ...

I've waited so long ... others have ...
He waits for me to stop and take a breath.

"Do you want to be healed?"
making no mention of the pool.

An Image of Prayer: Butterfly

Bursting from an egg,
the caterpillar begins to eat,
Always searching for food.
It eats, and eats, and eats
All the green leaves it can find.
Someone aptly called it "a crawling eater!"

With a burst of God into our lives,
our search for spiritual food in prayer
is endless.
Reflections, meditations, feeding the mind
with spiritual thoughts and images
become the green leaves of discursive prayer.

As the caterpillar eats, it grows and grows.
When it gets too big for its skin, it simply sheds it.
The new skin soon hardens itself to the caterpillar,
Not once but as often as it needed.
That repetition can be as many as five times!
Then it forms the outer shell of the chrysalis.

We need to shed so many things—
We keep shedding skins of prayer,
going from one form of prayer to another.
Prayer forms seem useless
as maturity marks our next adventure.

Secure in its chrysalis,
the caterpillar no longer searches for food
and seemingly has nothing to do!
Yet within this enclosure,
it is being transformed
into an adult butterfly. A masterpiece!

We grow in the darkness of a nada chrysalis,
where nothing seems to be happening in prayer.
But in this tomb-like darkness,
God is at work transforming our prayer!

The butterfly emerges!
A rebirth has taken place—the MONARCH!
To the delight of everyone.
But it cannot fly immediately.
The butterfly needs to rest and let the wings dry,
And it does this by pumping air
into the veins of its wings.
Then it is ready for flight.

When the time is ripe,
we too emerge from our chrysalis.
Moved now to more stillness, we rest,
we abide, just the occasional movement
of our wings of prayer, always in need of
the Spirit to pump fresh air into the veins
of our prayer-wings.

The butterfly in this new form of life
takes flight to all the waiting flowers
open for pollination!
This tiny creature affects the life
of many, many flowers.

In God's activity we fold and unfold the wings of prayer,
in rhythmic movement,
like a resting butterfly in adoring love.
Hardly can we imagine
the countless open flowers
awaiting the interactions of our prayer.
Presence and wings of prayer
are so very complementary!

Messengers of Love

The Incarnation of the Word Divine
The Angel Gabriel with zest now proclaims.
In love and faith, Mary does not decline,
For in her happy heart, God fully reigns.

When you are ill, God's remedy is near;
St Raphael will bring your illness to an end.
He'll journey with you, casting out your fear;
It's yours this healing spirit to befriend.

St Michael, prince of all the heavenly hosts,
E'er defending the love and truth of God,
With you I love to cry aloud and boast:
Who is like unto God?" I that applaud.

With incense floating up into refreshing air,
The angels journey on the wings of prayer.

Yellow Dandelions

Searching for nourishment, your roots go deep;
You multiply quickly while we are asleep.

With a spray they will feed you, hoping to kill,
But all their efforts are just about nil.

We know with certainty that it won't be long
You will come up again every bit as strong.

Just because you are born in the wrong place
You are looked upon with utter disgrace.

But then, in the tiny hands of innocent love,
You, O dandelion, are a real gift from above.

And mother is touched to receive such a gift
Now in a tall glass, it gives her a lift

Your strength to survive inspires me so,
Your colour a favourite of mine, I want you to know.

You are a symbol of my stance of real need.
O yellow dandelion, you're never a weed!

O Happy Dart

God's gift of friendship is alive in the heart,
as in the coolness of evening we walk.
Life has brought us together, ne'er to part;
In this blissful awareness, who wants to talk?

There in the delight to our eyes stood a tree;
Oh Happy Dart, you missed the mark.
And you, my soul, why did you flee
That friendship, that voice now painfully dark?

As God entered into a life-giving plan
When a baby was heard crying in the straw,
Here on this earth a new world began
That filled many a heart with heavenly awe.

No Precious Blood would have been shed,
Yet grace in a new wave did embark.
There would have been no Breaking of Bread,
If you, O Happy Dart, had not missed
that original mark!

The Precious Gift of Baptism

As a tiny bit of string,
I come to life,
only in the wax of the candle.

Once lit, I leap in the
joy and warmth of the wax.

In the abundance of wax,
my frail capacity is greatly felt.
In a large wax-well,
I flicker!
My light grows dim,
I bend, I lose my upward direction,
I fall.

In Your pruning touch,
I rise up and even glow
again and again.

In Your saving wax—
EVERYTHING.
Without it—STRING!

Lord, thank You for the gift of the candle
and not just string.

On Praise of Saskatchewan Winters!

Six months or so, we have an invasion;
Silently, softly settling everywhere,
The white flakes are every size and formation.
Winter wonderland, leaving nothing bare.
Pine trees' extended arms now filled with snow;
A sculpture of beauty before us lay.
Trees that stand frosted sentinels, just so,
While the wind has its say, howling away.
In crisp air, the Northern Lights come to play,
With waves of dancing colours that delight.
Behold! A very creative display
That fills the mind/soul in pondering height.
From the window I have a tranquil post;
To our loving Creator, I raise a toast!

Happiness Is...

Happy those blest
With furrows wide open,
Where seeds of grace flow
In a silence unbroken.

Happy those blest
Who in need of God thrive,
Just seeing a dandelion
Keeps this need alive.

Happy those blest
With an awareness of God,
So everything, everywhere
His presence applaud.

Happy those blest
when the soul feels so bare,
For the fruit of all this
Is the Gift of Prayer.

Vanity of Vanities

Oh! Vanities of vanities, says Qoheleth, who is bored.
O! Love, endless love, says Jesus, the Lord.

You, Lord, bring newness to everything under the sun.
And I gather that you, Qoheleth, do not know that fun.

There is lots of dignity in toil that's difficult to measure,
But the rest that follows is such a rich treasure.

Yes, generations are passing, but only on earth,
On the planet there are changes with every new birth.

Does the sun travel back and forth each day,
or is it the rotating earth that brings it on display?

O Holy Spirit, you're a spiraling life force
That changes north and south winds to send
them on course.

O Love, you keep us yearning for more and more,
Always you inspire us to reach your eternal shore.

Love, you know how to take all weariness out
So as to spark with life always ready to sprout.

You give "vision" to all our seeing,
The pleasure of listening to enrich our whole being.

What is and what has been and what is yet to come,
Describes Your Majesty; pray for Your will to be done.

Real news is not that which is flashed and spiced,
But the Good News is in the Gospel of Jesus Christ.

Remembrance is such treasures of heart and mind,
And in authentic prayer, no people are left behind.

(Inspired by Ecclesiastes 1)

My Lord and My God.

You, O God, are such an amazing Person!
So divine, so transcendent, yet
You remain our "ABBA."
Is it that you draw us up,
or it is that You come down?
Oh, those blessed moments of
transcendent love!
What an unbelievable treasure of my life
it is to discover
YOU—O TRIUNE GOD IN MY BEING,

*"... we will come to them and make
our home with them"* (John 14:23b, NRSV).

YET FAR GREATER TO DISCOVER
MY BEING IN YOU!

*"For in Him we live and move
and have our being"*
(Acts 17:28a).

Dandelion Thoughts

The desires of love are like dandelion weeds
Unless transformed in God's love and deeds.

Weeds all over the garden—that's bad!
Has sin imprisoned the Gardener I had?

Notes in my heart are taking their place
As the melody shapes my whole being with grace.

If I try to soar for higher things
Without accepting the clay of my wings,
My life will miss some essential links.

I told myself I could soar,
And I felt like it too,
But He had me picking violets
In a valley wet with dew

I tried to meditate
But my thoughts wouldn't penetrate.
I try nothing and contemplate,
And I love in a quiet state.

Cling, clang, listen to the sound
As my offerings fill the air!
"Pardon Me!

You'll have to lower your trumpet,
As it's drowning out your prayer."

How can I experience any real unity
As long as I keep eating off the same old tree?

I just can't measure
As I deeply treasure
The beautiful way
You came today!

I open my heart, and the bees soon invade,
To be stung from within even love starts to fade.
But without those bees no honey will be made.

I had a bright idea this noon.
In it I saw no flaw,
But when I shared it with the group,
It turned out to be straw. Aah!

I found out today how oysters make good use
Of pain and irritation, such fine pearls to produce.
Now I could do the same, if I wasn't such a goose

In the heat and the storm the dandelions grow.
But when the wind is strong, away they go!
The call to a depth, keeps searching within
To be grounded in faith and rooted in Him.

If in the yearning of my heart
The soundless voice of God I hear,
Yet to the cry of someone else,
I have no caring, listening ear.
I am a noisy gong that clangs
With love-sounds of a thin veneer.

DANDELION EXPERIENCES

To Adore, Suffer, and Repair

(Motto of the Institute of the
Sisters Adorers of the Precious Blood)

TO ADORE

Jesus is the perfect Adorer
Who goes into solitude to pray.
There to commune with His Father,
Until night dawns a new day.

I long to be humbly drawn
Into the Father's endless love
And into your prayer, O Jesus.
Of you, O God, I can't get enough.

TO SUFFER

From the cross, it's here you mirror
The love of an overflowing heart,
Where full of pain the sufferers gather,
Ever seeking a new life to start.

There is a longing in my soul
To help in a willing Cyrenian way,
With the cross of my brothers and sisters,
It's under his cross I stay.

TO REPAIR

In the pain of a broken relationship,
And it seems everything is falling apart,
Only Jesus can repair this damage,
His mercy and love to impart.

To be a compassionate listener
When someone's heart is breaking,
In prayer, to take them to Jesus,
Reparation is then in the making.

You are the ONE true Adorer
The ONE who bears the sufferings of us all
The only ONE who can repair what is broken
May I be a part of all this, in answer to my vocational call.

About the Author

I ENTERED THE Monastery of the Sisters of the Precious Blood in 1952. After living this vocation for over seventy years, I can honestly say that dedicating my life to God in the Monastery was the best decision I ever made, as my life has been happy and fulfilled. As a contemplative community, we have approximately four hours of daily formal prayer. Personal prayer is also vital to our growth as a community and as a child of God.

I have served in the community in many ways: as a Superior in various monasteries, as Formation Directress, and in the Secretary's office.

Our vocation to the contemplative life is a call to the ministry of intercessory prayer. How blessed are we when, with Jesus' compassion, we allow ourselves to feel the pain or need of those asking for our prayers.

Hundreds of letters with intentions come to us through the Secretary's office and by way of personal requests. Closely united with these friends, we bring these requests to our Eucharistic Lord and pray they may experience His loving, compassionate presence and a favourable answer.

As a young child, I was paralyzed with poliomyelitis. Though often physically challenged, I was up and around (though not up and running), until I fell and broke my frail polio-affected leg almost beyond repair. Thus, at age sixty-five, I began my life in a wheelchair with an entire leg brace. Since I know from experiential knowledge what it means to be physically challenged, I keep a special remembrance of all those who suffer from any physical affliction in my prayers.

This book of poems is an expression of treasured moments of my life. I hope and pray that you too have many of these.